اب ناشتے کا وقت ہے۔ آپ کیا کھائیں گے؟

It's time for breakfast.

What will you eat?

3

کیا آپ کورن فلیکس دودھ کے ساتھ لیں گے؟

Will you put milk on cornflakes?

یا پھر کوئی میٹھی چیز لیں گے؟

Or will you grab something sweet?

کھانے سے گند بھی پڑ سکتا ہے۔

Eating can be messy.

اس طرح کرنے سے مزہ بھی آتا ہے۔

It's also fun to do.

اپنے ہاتھ دھولیں۔ شکر ادا کریں۔

Wash your hands. Give thanks.

پسر کھانا شروع کریں!

Then dig into your food!

آپ میز پر بیٹھ کر کھا سکتے ہیں،

You can eat at a table,

اور زمین پر بھی،

on the ground,

یا بھاگتے ہوئے بھی۔

or on the run.

لیکن اس سے پہلے کہ آپ کھانا کھائیں،
بہت سے کام کرنے ہوتے ہیں۔

But before you can eat,
there's a lot to be done.

آپ خوراک خریدیں یا خود اگائیں۔

Buy food or grow it.

پھر اسے پیس لیں یا الگ الگ کر لیں۔

Then, pound it or sort it.

کاٹ لیں اور پھر ہلائیں۔

Chop it, then stir it.

پھر اسے گرل کریں یا دیگچی میں پکائیں۔

Grill it on a fire or cook it in a pot.

غذا کا بہت مزہ آتا ہے ۔ بعض اوقات گرم ہوتی ہے۔
بعض اوقات نہیں۔

Food tastes great—sometimes hot,
sometimes not.

جب آپ اکٹھے مل کر کھانا کھاتے ہیں،
اس سے بہت مزہ آتا ہے اور وقت بھی اچھا گزر جاتا ہے۔

When you share a meal,
you share good tastes and good times.

آرام سے بیٹھ جاؤ۔ اور ایک بہت بڑا لقمہ لو !

Sit right down. Take a big bite!

کھانا کھانے سے آپ بہت اچھا محسوس کرتے ہیں۔

Eating will make you feel just right.

More about the Pictures

Front cover: Peanut butter on bread makes for fun but messy eating for this boy in Ann Arbor, Michigan.

Back cover: A girl in the Philippines carries a big bowl full of bananas.

Page 1: Two boys in Guyana, in South America, slurp flavoured ice cones.

Page 3: For this toddler in northern India, breakfast starts with a bottle of milk.

Page 4: This young girl in Cantonment, Florida, begins the day with a bowl of cornflakes.

Page 5: At a market in Toluca, Mexico, children eat sweet, ripe bananas.

Page 6: In Scotland, a toddler tastes—and wears—chocolate.

Page 7: Two English schoolgirls stop for a spaghetti lunch.

Page 8: Young children in Hong Kong say grace before eating.

Page 9: These boys in Morocco, in northwest Africa, use their hands to eat couscous topped with vegetables and meat.

Page 10: Women on a trip to Antarctica eat lunch on their ship.

Page 11: Kids on a field trip to the George Washington Carver National Monument in Missouri take a lunch break.

Page 12: A student on the go in Ho Chi Minh City, Vietnam, eats a quick snack.

Page 13: In Puttaparthi, India, a boy brings home a basket of tomatoes to cook.

Page 14: A teacher shows off the vegetables she has grown in Malawi, a country in southeastern Africa.

Page 15: A woman in Nigeria, in West Africa, removes cocoa beans from their pods.

Page 16: It's time to chop onions in this kitchen in Chisinau, Moldova.

Page 17: Women in Ghana, a country in West Africa, make smoked herring on a grill.

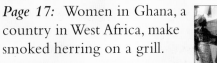

Page 18: At a shelter for homeless children in Bangkok, Thailand, children get a hot meal.

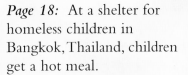

Page 19: A teacher in Fort Simpson, in the Northwest Territories, shows native Canadian girls how to make hot dogs covered with bannock, a kind of bread.

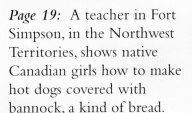

Page 20: A child from a hill tribe in Tamil Nadu, India, sits down to eat.

Page 21: In Paris, France, a mother and son share some mealtime fun.

A Note to Adults on Sharing This Book

Help your child become a lifelong reader. Read this book together, taking turns as you both read out loud. Look over the photographs and choose your favourites. Sound out new words and come back to them later for review. Then try these "extensions"—activities that extend the experience of reading and build discussion and problem-solving skills.

Talk about Eating

All around the world, you can find people eating. Discuss with your child the kinds of foods people eat in different countries. Where do you get the food you eat? Where do people in other parts of the world get their food? What ways of preparing food are shown in this book?

Make a Food Chart

With your child, draw pictures of the foods you both love to eat. Find pictures of your favourite foods in magazines. Then find out where your favourite foods fit on the food pyramid. Which of your favourite foods should you eat less of—or more of—in order to be healthy?

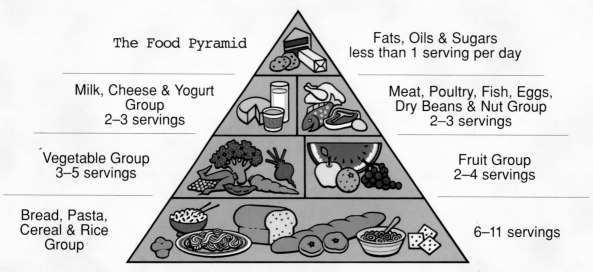

The Food Pyramid

Fats, Oils & Sugars
less than 1 serving per day

Milk, Cheese & Yogurt
Group
2–3 servings

Meat, Poultry, Fish, Eggs,
Dry Beans & Nut Group
2–3 servings

Vegetable Group
3–5 servings

Fruit Group
2–4 servings

Bread, Pasta,
Cereal & Rice
Group

6–11 servings